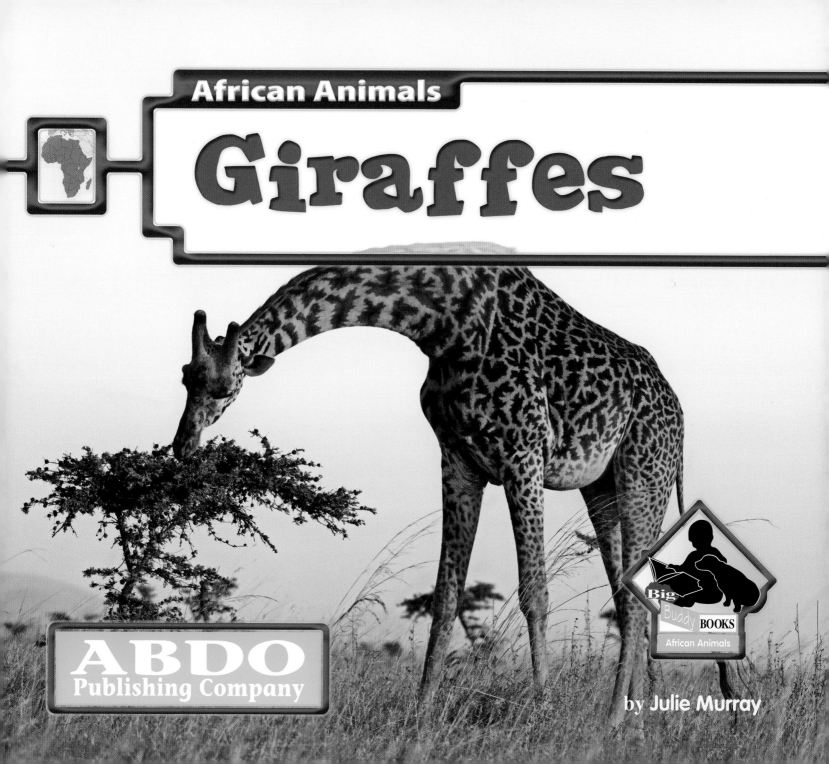

African Animals

Giraffes

ABDO
Publishing Company

by Julie Murray

Big
Buddy BOOKS
African Animals

VISIT US AT

www.abdopublishing.com

Published by ABDO Publishing Company, PO Box 398166, Minneapolis, MN 55439.

Copyright © 2012 by Abdo Consulting Group, Inc. International copyrights reserved in all countries. No part of this book may be reproduced in any form without written permission from the publisher. Big Buddy Books™ is a trademark and logo of ABDO Publishing Company.

Printed in the United States of America, North Mankato, Minnesota.
102011
012012

PRINTED ON RECYCLED PAPER

Coordinating Series Editor: Rochelle Baltzer
Editor: Marcia Zappa
Contributing Editors: Megan M. Gunderson, BreAnn Rumsch, Sarah Tieck
Graphic Design: Maria Hosley
Cover Photograph: *iStockphoto*: ©iStockphoto.com/WLDavies.
Interior Photographs/Illustrations: *Corbis* (pp. 8, 11); *Eyewire* (p. 8); *iStockphoto*: ©iStockphoto.com/brytta
    (p. 4), ©iStockphoto.com/PTB-images (p. 4); *Photolibrary*: Age fotostock (p. 10), Bios (p. 25), Imagebroker.
    net (p. 25), Japan Travel Bureau (p. 17), Oxford Scientific (OSF) (p. 23), Peter Arnold Images (pp. 7, 19, 21, 25);
    Shutterstock: Henk Beatlage (p. 27), Eric Eisnaagle (p. 9), Lenice Harms (p. 17), Ivan Cholakav Gostock-dot-net
    (p. 27), Martin Kraft (p. 14), Andrea Little (p. 29), Christian Musat (p. 15), Anna Omelchenko (p. 13), palko72
    (p. 19), Albie Venter (p. 13), Oleg Znameskiy (p. 9); *Stockbyte* (p. 5).

Library of Congress Cataloging-in-Publication Data

Murray, Julie, 1969-
  Giraffes / Julie Murray.
      p. cm. -- (African animals)
  ISBN 978-1-61783-219-2
  1. Giraffe--Juvenile literature. I. Title.
  QL737.U56M875 2012
  599.638--dc23
                                    2011027845

Contents

Long ago, nearly all land on Earth was one big mass. About 200 million years ago, the land began to break into **continents**. One of these is called Africa.

Giraffes are the tallest land animals on Earth. They are known for their long necks and patchlike markings.

Africa is the second-largest **continent**. It is known for hot weather, wild land, and interesting animals. One of these animals is the giraffe. In the wild, giraffes are only found in Africa.

Giraffe Territory

There are nine types of giraffes. All live in Africa south of the Sahara Desert.

Giraffes are most common in eastern Africa and parts of southern Africa. They live in dry, open areas. These include **savannas** and woodlands.

SAHARA DESERT

Nile River

Giraffe Territory

Giraffes share Africa's savannas with animals such as zebras and kudu.

Jambo! Welcome to Africa!

If you took a trip to where giraffes live, you might find…

…many languages.

More than 1,000 languages are spoken across Africa! Swahili (swah-HEE-lee) is common in eastern Africa where many giraffes live. In Swahili, *jambo* is a greeting for visitors. *Masalala* means "goodness!" or "wow!" And *twiga* means "giraffe."

…hot weather.

Almost 90 percent of Africa is in the tropics! The tropics is the area near Earth's equator. It is warm there all year, even in winter!

...acacia plants.

Acacia trees and bushes grow in warm areas around the world. They are common on Africa's savannas. And, their leaves are a favorite meal of giraffes.

...many different groups of people.

Africa is made up of 54 countries. Most of these have several groups of people within them. These groups each have their own histories and ways of life.

Great Heights

Giraffes are large animals. Males can grow more than 18 feet (5.5 m) tall. They weigh up to 4,200 pounds (1,900 kg). Females can grow more than 14 feet (4.3 m) tall. They weigh up to 2,500 pounds (1,100 kg).

Giraffes need big feet to support their large bodies. Each foot is as big around as a dinner plate!

Giraffes tower over humans, animals, and many trees.

A giraffe's neck weighs about 600 pounds (270 kg).

Most of a giraffe's height comes from its long legs and neck. Each is about six feet (1.8 m) long.

A giraffe's neck has just seven bones. That's the same number as a human's neck has! But, a giraffe's bones are much bigger. Each one can be more than ten inches (25 cm) long.

Having only seven long neck bones makes a giraffe's neck stiff. So, it isn't easy for giraffes to bend down. To reach drinking water, they must move their legs far apart.

Take a Closer Look

Giraffes have thin bodies and sloping backs. Their small heads have large eyes and ears. They also have at least two short knobs on top of their heads. These knobs are made of bone and covered in skin and hair.

A giraffe's tail is short compared to its body. It is only about three feet (1 m) long.

A giraffe's knobs help guard its head during fights. They can grow to be about five inches (13 cm) long.

Uncovered!

Many scientists believe that a giraffe's pattern helps it blend in with trees.

Giraffes are covered in short, thick fur. They have short manes on the backs of their necks. And their tails end in long, black hairs.

A giraffe's fur has blackish, brown, or brownish-yellow patches. The patches are separated by tan or white lines. No two giraffes have exactly the same pattern. But, giraffes of the same type look similar.

Some giraffes have big patches separated by thin white lines. Some people say these giraffes look like they have been caught in a net.

Mealtime

Most animals can't reach food high in trees. But giraffes can! They eat leaves, twigs, and fruit. Their most common meal is acacia tree leaves.

A giraffe spends many hours each day eating and chewing. After a giraffe's meal reaches its stomach, the food returns to its mouth for more chewing. This partly **digested** food is called cud.

Giraffes get most of the water they need from their food. So, they can go for many weeks without drinking water.

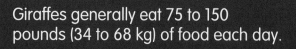

Giraffes generally eat 75 to 150 pounds (34 to 68 kg) of food each day.

A giraffe gathers food using its upper lip and tongue. A giraffe's tongue can be about 21 inches (53 cm) long! It has **muscles** that allow it to grab and hold objects.

Acacia trees have sharp thorns. So, many animals can't eat from them. But, giraffes use their long tongues to reach around thorns. They have thick, sticky **saliva** that coats food they eat. This guards giraffes from any thorns they might eat by mistake.

A giraffe's tongue is dark blue or black. Many people believe this helps keep it from getting sunburned.

Herd Life

Giraffes are **social** animals. They live in small, open herds. Giraffe herds have no leaders, and giraffes come and go freely. Herds usually have up to 20 giraffes. Females and their young form herds. Groups of young males also form herds. Older males join herds from time to time. But, they usually live alone.

Uncovered!

Giraffes are usually quiet, but they do make noises sometimes. They whistle, snort, moo, hiss, and roar. Giraffes also make very low sounds that cannot be heard by people.

Living in a herd helps giraffes stay safe. Herd members often take turns resting and drinking. That way, at least one giraffe is always watching for predators.

Staying Safe

Adult giraffes have few predators. Their size usually keeps them away. But animals such as lions and crocodiles hunt young giraffes. Even adults are at risk when they lie down to rest or bend down to drink. That is because they are so slow to get back up!

Still, adult giraffes have ways to stay safe. Their height and good eyesight help them spot predators from far away. Their long, powerful legs let them quickly run away or kick hard.

A strong kick from a giraffe can kill a lion!

Giraffes walk slowly, but they run fast! They can run up to 35 miles (56 km) per hour!

Female giraffes protect their young by standing over them. They kick any predators that come near.

25

Baby Giraffes

Giraffes are **mammals**. Female giraffes usually have one baby at a time. Baby giraffes are called calves. At birth, they are already about six feet (1.8 m) tall! And, they can weigh about 150 pounds (68 kg).

A newborn calf drinks its mother's milk. After two to three weeks, it starts eating leaves. About one to two years later, a young giraffe is ready to live without its mother.

At first, a calf stays close to its mother. Later, it stays in a group with other young giraffes when its mother leaves to find food.

Baby giraffes grow very fast. They can grow four feet (1.2 m) in their first year!

Uncovered!

Female giraffes give birth standing up. So, newborns often fall five to six feet (1.5 to 1.8 m) to the ground!

Survivors

Life in Africa isn't easy for giraffes. New buildings and farms take over their **habitats**. And, humans hunt giraffes for their meat, their skin, and the hair on their tails.

Still, giraffes **survive**. Scientists consider most types of giraffes stable. And, many people are working to save their habitats. Giraffes help make Africa an amazing place!

In the wild, giraffes live up to 25 years.

Masalala!
I'll bet you never knew...

...that giraffes often sleep standing up. That way, they are ready for danger.

...that giraffes can close their noses. This keeps out sand and dust.

...that long ago people called giraffes "camel-leopards." They saw the bump on a giraffe's back and the patches on its coat. They thought it was a combination of a camel and a leopard!

...that there is only one other animal closely related to the giraffe. It is the okapi, which has a body like a horse. Okapis are uncommon animals. In the wild, they are only found in Africa.

Important Words

continent one of Earth's seven main land areas.

digest (deye-JEHST) to break down food into parts small enough for the body to use.

habitat a place where a living thing is naturally found.

mammal a member of a group of living beings. Mammals make milk to feed their babies and usually have hair or fur on their skin.

muscles (MUH-suhls) body tissues, or layers of cells, that help move the body.

saliva a liquid produced by the body that keeps the mouth moist.

savanna a grassy plain with few or no trees.

social (SOH-shuhl) naturally living or growing in groups.

survive to continue to live or exist.

Web Sites

To learn more about giraffes, visit ABDO Publishing Company online. Web sites about giraffes are featured on our Book Links page. These links are routinely monitored and updated to provide the most current information available.

www.abdopublishing.com

Index